10 MAJOR EVENTS NO ONE SAW COMING

SYDNEY HUGHES

CONTENTS

ACKNOWLEDGMENTS

To my wife, Pixie, without whom this book could not have been completed. She is not only an encourager, but a master in the process of "the how" when it comes to bringing thought to expression in print.

To Kathy, a true friend and insightful and talented typist.

And to Melissa, our committed and extremely busy daughter who kept me on track and found the time to edit, refine, and produce the draft copy ready for publication.

To Chris, Andrea and Rebecca who brought together their expertise in formatting and page by page checked to see it was readable from a contemporary point of view.

And Peter, my friend, scholar, book publisher and accredited teacher who studied the manuscript. True to his profession, he has enabled a rounded perspective, especially in areas, where differing views are often expressed.

To my friend and artist Noel.

My enthusiastic grandchildren, Joel and Brianna, who have greatly encouraged the project to reach finalisation.

Thank you Kevin, your valued editing and publishing experience has seen this book through to its final completion in print and e-book form.

PREFACE

To quote an ancient saying, "there is nothing like a good dose of reality to produce a healthy respect for evidence". Whilst bad news and serious conflicts often crowd the air waves, a global reality is that in the last two generations there have been no world wars.

Abundance and growing prosperity have been the order of the day for some, yet for others the very basics of life are only a mirage.

Regardless, the pace of change is rapid, and whether there is abundance or lack thereof, a growing cross section of the human race from all sides are asking, "is part of being human having to always be on the search for more meaning or indeed any meaning to life?" A good question! Is there a good answer?

Having lived a relatively busy life, I have found the "more", in fact more than could be imagined – better than gold it's true!

As we undertake this journey together, may it lead you to discover the peace, love and security I have come to know for over 60 years. Along life's journey, although from differing backgrounds, I've met many fellow travellers who, likewise, identify with my experience.

The circumstances of life may seem to produce more questions than answers, but it is far too important to reduce it to a guessing game, nothingness, or pie in the sky when you die. Say 'no' to darkness – and say 'yes' to the light.

In your quest for a full life, I trust that this book will lead you on the pathway which answers your deepest need.

1

TEN MAJOR EVENTS ON THE EARTH

There have been ten major events that forever changed our world, but no one saw them coming! If you think you have heard of these already, I suggest that you almost certainly have not. Indeed, you are not likely to hear about these major events in the public domain.

The entertainment and communication media that now continually bombards us, leaves us feeling overwhelmed and confused. In fact, one wonders whether these increasingly pervasive and intrusive voices are subtly undermining our values, subverting our wills and threatening the very freedoms that we have taken for granted.

So don't shut the book; take a closer look. History tells us if we don't learn the lessons it can teach, we are more likely to repeat its many mistakes. These history topics are therefore massively important and most of us know little or nothing about them. We can all agree, however, with the way things stand, despite scientific advance and great increase in knowledge, our world is in trouble. Is there a way forward? Is there any 'right' way? With so many choices and differing viewpoints, how can anyone know?

At the forefront, world leaders and world planners agree that the future is not looking good for the earth and its inhabitants.

They even think that unless action is taken and quickly, it could easily end where it all started much sooner than we may realise – 'ground zero'. These leaders have engaged 'think tanks' and are well underway to see if they can design, organise, and restructure society in such a way as to future proof our race from an otherwise threatening calamity. Some are alarmed while others appear to show signs of panic. Personally, I'm not a fear driver, but the reality is that in the 21st century, vast areas have known famine with malnutrition and starvation, serious fires and floods, earthquakes and tsunamis, massive volcanic eruptions, and a global pandemic. In addition, we have a plethora of unprecedented social conflicts such as gender, sexuality, race, climate etc. Nations have been facing off against each other, testing their resolve and might. The possibility of another global conflict with apocalyptic consequences is always nearby. The result of modern major warfare engagement, places us all in uncharted territory. Each event discussed in this book is like a signpost, pointing to a vital message! Yet every one of them has been largely overlooked. If you take the time now, you will see for yourself the cost to our human race in the previous eras and the way this cost could have been avoided, even turned in a positive way, had our forebears listened.

Continuously we are told we live in a global village as never before. We need, therefore, to think differently and act not so much as independent operatives as we have previously. This, we are told, is because we have expressions of many different and often competing visions. We are 'all in this together' and need to move forward; we will have to, as nations, pull together in a unified way. We all agree with this, but how? A combination of these factors sets the stage for a new global system:

1. The way things have been done in the past will have to change.
2. Previously accepted social fabric and constructs must change to conform with a new global order.
3. The distribution of resources must be addressed as the once accepted economic market - led belief has produced a glaring discrepancy between respective people groups, commonly known as 'haves' and 'have nots'.

Many planners with their in-depth structural changes for society are already gearing up, but in principle their plan can be summed up under their especially designed slogan **deconstruct** what is existing and **build back better**. Further, they say that humanity is strong, resilient and can achieve whatever is needed. Time is running, out they say, but there is a window of opportunity, and the world will have to move with speed. This they assure us, will benefit everyone; together we can build back better – a new global reset.

But what to do with the ten major events discussed in this book. Easy, they say, let's use cancel culture through modern media to effectively suppress its message. Let this be the *new normal* for everything that is neither wanted nor needed. However, in ancient times and even recently, haven't other names been used to illustrate the result of doing this. For example: *ignore the facts at your peril?* Regardless of the slogan used, none have worked before, so why should we expect them to work, just because we are in the 21st century with a newly invented slogan.

Nevertheless, in schools, universities, corporations and government bodies, momentum for this cancel culture is gaining traction every day. Its replacement, when closely examined, is the same old socialism leading to communism, but for our modern society, it's wearing new clothes. It sounds convincing, dressed in the new lingo, but every time civilizations went away from the truth devastating consequences have been the result. Every nation in history that departed from truth in past generations has either disappeared or become greatly diminished, even though at the time they wielded power, their day in the sunshine looked endless.

The idea that events which changed the course of history do not matter now or did not happen, should alarm everyone. Instead, most of us are oblivious, occupied with everyday affairs, and so this new way of thinking has been normalized largely under the radar. Was anyone listening when their previously strong civilizations based upon false philosophy became brittle and then vanished into thin air before? No. Is anyone listening now? No. Do we need to listen? We certainly do!

If we will not listen when there is danger, the result is often disastrous. Only the truth can make us free, but what is truth? So please take a few minutes to look, listen and consider a change in thinking. May that change be in accord with the truth, which does not alter and is not governed by any quick convenience of this current 'now' generation. True change for the good in even just one person can result in benefits to many far and wide. In reading further, you may find that change for the good is for you.

2

A GREAT START - MAJOR EVENT 1

THE FIRST MAJOR EVENT

When this event happened, none of us were there, however the complexity, balance, and beauty over eons of time speak louder and louder every day. Every design needs a designer. It is plain logic. [1]"Let us make man in our image and likeness", said Creator God, the God of Life – so He made them male and female. Generally speaking, now, we don't want anything involving God, so bring on evolution instead. Do not say creation, say evolution; say everything is evolving.

A large body of science today is saying evolution isn't working and that it is not science, but 'think tanks' are still saying it is excellent because it doesn't need God. More importantly, evolution is convenient because it can leave God out, which assists in a secular education and society at large. So, our way of addressing the answer we think we need to come up with at present is to keep teaching this increasingly dubious evolutionary theory, especially to children in school and university – call it science when it isn't and give it unlimited public funds. Focus on dinosaurs and millions of years, even though dating formulas that are used are variable and wildly contested, they will listen and love it! The funds used to prop up what is sheer guess work theory may appear to be a waste of money but for the evolutionist there is an upside, because it's effective in keeping people from thinking about God.

There are many examples of this guess work theory not making sense, but just consider for a moment transitionary fossils. None have ever been found, yet complete fossils are located across the globe. If evolution were true science, you would expect to have fossils evolving in transition, found across the earth just as fully formed fossils are found everywhere. In all the years since Charles Darwin, with study, excavations, and billions of dollars spent, not one uncontested transitional fossil has been found. Each fossil located anywhere on earth is seen to be complete within itself and non-transitional. If Darwin were expounding his theory today, he would not get to first base, and said so himself: if there is no transition fossil, it remains a theory. Remember, when evolution landed on the planet a relatively short time ago, the evolutionist's goal was no God needed and this hasn't changed. In the end, how can a theory based on guess work be trusted just because it's believed by some scientists and propped up by huge public funds, with people being paid handsomely to continue what is essentially a guessing game?

Why is evolution harmful you ask? It is because people, especially children, miss the truth that God is the author of all life and, in particular, humanity – this is a big miss. Regardless, many educationalists prefer the unsettled science of evolution to be taught just because it fits the current secular ideology. Generally speaking, they do not present the alternative of God in creation even for consideration, inferring that he probably doesn't exist or is irrelevant. Indoctrination of this nature results in doubt or a closed mind toward God.

CATASTROPHIC END - MAJOR EVENT 2

THE SECOND MAJOR EVENT

For this event you and I weren't there either. However, people were. We are told by God that, unfortunately, because the creation decided to go against His good plan in favour of their own way, there developed a world full of violence and prideful greedy humanity [1] God says that our good idea to make mankind is not working - it is going nowhere and becoming intolerable, we will have to end it. Then a man warned by God that a great flood was coming was instructed to build a life saving boat. He was convicted to do this even though it was out near the desert in the Middle East. It was not a cruise liner, but one made for some people and animals - it did the job. The dimensions given we are told are about the size of the famous English vessel, the Queen Mary.

People scoffed: silly old Noah! Many years passed while he kept building, as he continued to say a flood is coming; it will be serious. He was constantly challenged but was certain that what he had heard was true. Eventually the mocking and curious public saw animals streaming in – how ridiculous it all would have looked. They then witnessed old Noah's family go in and laughed. But then the flood came and took them all away, except for "silly old Noah" and those on his big boat. It was more serious than could have been imagined- scoffing ended, laughing ended, and all ended – but no one could say it came without warning.

Where did Noah get the knowledge to build this thing? It had been built to an exact size and dimensions and by any standard of the then known world, it was huge. A big trouble equals a big warning for future generations. [2]Didn't God show clearly that a flood was coming? Didn't he also demonstrate that he had completely rejected mankind's violence, pride and disregard for him and his creation? Was anyone listening ? No, as it suited that generation to ignore the true Word, so they could get on with what they perceived as everyday life. Later in the book we are going to consider some of the responses from recent and present generations to this particular record, however for the moment, let us continue with the narrative.

4

UNFINISHED PROJECT - MAJOR EVENT 3

THE THIRD MAJOR EVENT

After the flood, there could now be a brand-new start. God said, "Go out and prosper and populate the earth." Great news - a new beginning! Vast wide-open spaces, no more violence, and no one to say – you can't go there. People started to populate again: the generations and years passed. All good. No, not exactly! [1]Instead of the wide-open spaces, people said, let's stick together, that way we can be strong, united, big and beautiful – we can build a very high tower to show it, and the catch-cry came again – whoever God may or may not be, we don't have a need. The human race is becoming prideful again. When God speaks, He says one thing - we say something different. Instead, people said, by building a great tower, we can demonstrate our fantastic humanity.

[2]So God said: They are not spreading across the earth to their benefit, there will be no stopping of endless and futile human self-promotion. We will change their speech from one language to many different ones. The result was that suddenly and without warning many languages transpired. Tower building

immediately stopped; people could not understand one another.

After coming to grips with this new dynamic which changed everything for early humanity, people found each language group, banded together in their groups by language and went out finally spreading across and populating the earth. [3]Didn't God say to go and do this very thing? This total restructure could be reckoned as an account worth listening to, but what is humanities response to this massive population shift? This is covered further into the events, but basically it has been to deny its authenticity. This may appear to be inconsequential, but further into this book, it will be seen that our world is moving on and God is the true instigator, while most are asleep to the reality. Who is listening?

PEOPLE ON THE MOVE - MAJOR EVENT 4

THE FOURTH MAJOR EVENT

After moving in separate ways because of this newly acquired language barrier, the human race began populating across a wide area, with daily life returning to their socially accepted norm. There was sometimes a little violence and sometimes a lot of violence – some groups became more powerful and some less. People designed gods for their communities as required. Each generation lived for a while, sometimes fighting over lands, sometimes fighting each other with the next generation doing much the same thing which covered a period of several thousand years. Nevertheless, despite all that had been in the previous eras – creation, flood and language barrier, the new societies carried the weight of their own way, with what they thought best into each generation.

[1]God said they can still get to know me because the earth shows my handiwork, and the heavens (universe) speak of my glory. There is no place where my name cannot be known. Nevertheless, increasingly people preferred idols which could at best inspire them to be like these inanimate images. [2]God

said that while humans think they are on an improving and upward-moving culture, they've become corrupt, having exchanged my glory for these worthless images. Could it be thought of as an affront to the God of Life? The very reverse of His Good Plan.

All dating techniques for early man are highly suspect and equally questionable. They are determined by theory and modelling, all of which carry huge variations. Decisions have to be taken regarding which theory and which model will be used, but in most fields, the currently popular theory is taught as accepted fact.

(**Note:** The modern versions of dictatorship, communism, Eastern and Western plans with revisions, may have worked to free societies from ancient negative customs by coercion, force or democratic occupations, but each person individually still has a longing to be free. Freedom remains the driving force in each human being, so why is it elusive, and why is it searched for in so many places – many of them wrong places?)

THE INTERNATIONAL CONNECTION - MAJOR EVENT 5

THE FIFTH MAJOR EVENT

No one could have imagined any change as it looked like the eternal human norm was set. However, for one Middle Eastern nation, the focus started to become a little different, because God said, [1]"Through this nation I am going to speak to the world." Starting with Abraham and his wife Sarah, who believed God, they were directed to go as foreigners to the land which is now called Israel. [2]They had two sons, Isaac and Ishmael, and this is the reason why most Middle Eastern nations claim Abraham as their father. Isaac was the father of the Jewish line and Ishmael all others. [3]Then Isaac had two sons also – twins Jacob and Esau. Again [4]Jacob, whose name was changed to Israel by God, was the father of the Jewish line and Esau all others. [5]Jacob had 12 sons, and his favourite son was Joseph.

There was sibling rivalry to the point where Joseph was hated by his brothers. They despised him so much, they prepared to kill him one day, but at the last minute, decided instead to sell him to a passing band of Arab traders who took him to Egypt and sold him for slave money there. ⁶It looked like the end for Joseph (a worthless slave), but he had three outstanding attributes. He was a good listener, was very astute, could interpret dreams accurately – and these life qualities changed everything. We could do well to pause here and repeat – a good listener.

These were recognized by the king, when one night, he had a very bad dream. In it, he saw great prosperity and incredible poverty. In his dream, the prosperity was totally wiped out by what followed. ⁷Joseph was called in and was able to tell the king what the dream meant for this king and for Egypt – which he ruled. Joseph said seven years of mass produce would be followed by seven shocking years of inconceivable and unrelenting drought. Amazingly, unlike others before him, this king was listening! Although as Pharaoh, King of Egypt, he was considered to be a god, he must have known his limitations. He believed Joseph's interpretation and, acting wisely, put him in charge of building store houses for grain etc., so they would be ready for the bad times coming. ⁸He made Joseph the controller of store houses, and ruler of Egypt next to Pharaoh.

Back in the bush, after years of watching carelessly as their sad father Jacob tried to deal with his eleven sons' cover-up story of his son Joseph being eaten by a wild animal, the same serious drought as in Egypt was biting those brothers and they and their families were starving. Their best hope was, if possible, to buy the only available food from Egypt, so they set off and later arrived there. ⁹After an agonizingly touching and deeply moving family conversation with their long-lost brother Joseph, there was a wonderful reconciliation and reunion. (Imagine, the brothers had no idea it was their once hated sibling whom they thought they were rid of forever, and now was the very person they were negotiating with to buy food.) He was dressed in royal robes and spoke in

Egyptian. [10]Though they didn't know it, he knew it was his brothers.

After this gut wrenching and emotionally traumatic experience of having to deal with his brothers whom he knew would once have easily murdered him, he forgave them and invited them to come down to live in Egypt and enjoy all the provisions with the blessing of the king. Joseph said, go home and when you come again, don't forget to bring our father. The famine ended and all went well for this generation and a number of subsequent generations. As far as they were concerned, they were cared for in Egypt, prospered there and it could have remained that way forever.

[11]In later generations however, Egyptian kings became terrified by the rapidly increasing Jewish population living in their land, so they decided to control them by enslaving them all. Egypt's kings and queens loved pyramids and sphinx, they were the latest craze and an excellent status symbol, so, 'win-win', cheap labour and absolute control is the answer for our nation, they said. It went that way for around 450 years and seemed as though the constant making and carrying of bricks would never change for this slave race, **but** then [12]God said: I am going to fulfil the promise I made to Abraham and give his descendants the land I sent him to – the land of Israel. No more of this; their Egyptian slavery is ended. It's one thing to say it, but the doing of it is another.

How could this happen? This nation of slaves to be made free? You would have to be joking! But then [13]God is speaking, and He says, remember when I open a door, no one shuts it and when I close a door, no one opens it. We are going to get an insight into what happens when adamantly someone, even a king who is told he is god, decides to go up against the true God.

SLAVERY TO FREEDOM - MAJOR EVENT 6

THE SIXTH MAJOR EVENT

God, then as now, has unique ways of achieving his purpose. As he says, speaking to his creation – [1]"my way is not your way, and my thoughts are not your thoughts." God selected an 80-year-old man to lead them out of Egypt - a Jew named Moses who had run away as a fugitive from that country 40 years earlier. When he was born, to reduce the population, Pharaoh issued an edict to kill all the baby boys.

Moses was saved when his mother put him in a basket in the Nile River and, ultimately, he was found by Pharaoh's daughter who raised him as a prince in the king's court. However, things went badly for him and at 40 years of age he had to go into hiding and build another life, (he was never going back to Egypt). Now aged, having well and truly settled into his other life in the desert, he had no vision of being a hero. [2]He listened to God's idea but said: "I don't want to have any part of Jews getting out of Egypt". God said to him: "Don't worry, with me on your side, everything will work well". [3]Quite emphatically, Moses still said: "No!" However, when his brother, who lived in

Egypt, said he would do the talking to the king on Moses' behalf, he finally agreed.

After huge yet anticipated obstructions from Egypt's king, it happened as God had said. As we now know from history, the enslaved Jews left Egypt. The cost to this Egyptian king was enormous, as he would not listen. He had no intention of losing slaves and he would not agree to give up his brick makers for anything until the entire nation had been impoverished: all his productive lands were destroyed, the fertile Nile River was fouled with dead fish, sick Egyptians were everywhere across his lands, his army was decimated and ultimately all the prized Egyptian children, the firstborn from every family (including the king's family) died in a single night. Basically, plague after plague struck Egypt until, suffering unimaginable trauma, the king said to Moses, "Just go! and take with you whatever of ours you want".

Now we would not believe what happened next - but we should! Greed and power can be a hard and cruel task master and this king was about to learn a serious and horrendous lesson. [4]He suddenly began to have remorse at his loss of slaves. Remember he was always considered to be an all-powerful god and so he decided against all the wisdom you could believe or imagine, to change his mind. "Get those Slaves back!" he said to his invincible army. "No worries! They are just a disorganized rabble; they will be stopped by the Red Sea. We will get them. See you soon, and be back home with the slaves, you only thought you had lost them" they replied.

The Jews heard the army coming, but Moses said to the fearful ex slaves, [5]"Watch God's deliverance". The wind blew hard, and a pathway opened across the Red Sea which had previously blocked their way forward. Moses said: "Get on the pathway and cross now while you can". Through they went until they all reached the other side. (It is estimated that around 1 million slave Jews crossed at that time). Go after them, said the army commanders. Make it quick while this wind keeps blowing. So, they got on the pathway. Once they were all in and crossing-chariots, horses, commanders, and soldiers - it happened! You've possibly heard about it: wind stopped blowing, sea closed in, army all drowned and became washed up dead on the seashore – no one left alive, not one. The Jews saw the awesome power of Creator God. It's an event that resonated across the then known world. They were free for the first time in 450 years.

But were they really free? What about their desire for their own way with no "God bothering"? It's a strong condition in every human being by nature: more on that shortly. So started the new nation toward the land of Israel. They went with Moses for 40 years in a roundabout fashion toward the promised land and finally the next generation under Joshua, their new leader and military general, crossed the Jordan River to occupy Israel, then called the Land of Canaan. This is the same land that Israel occupies today. It's also the same land God sent Abraham to live in, but in a tent then, as well as Isaac and Jacob also in tents during their life- time.

To anyone listening, there are many insightful points about this land, God's authority, and impeccable planning. For example, Abraham and his wife, Sarah, after leaving their homeland in Ur, finally settled in Canaan (Israel) and were buried there. Jacob, even though he died in Egypt with great honour after Joseph brought him there when he ruled Egypt during the famine, was taken back to Israel for burial, and Joseph, the brother, sold as slave who became the ruler of Egypt, when he was dying said: [6]"God will one day take you out of this land and when he does, make sure my bones go with you."

[7]When the Jews left Egypt, hundreds of years later, they took his bones with them and he was buried at last in Israel. By the way, Jesus Christ was also born in this land; what a story! So here they are, freedom from slavery, and a beautiful land to occupy and live in. Fabulous, freedom, land, money, houses etc. But No! Because, in the end, when they had everything they could ever dream of and more, they stopped listening to the very One who had given it all to them. In all honesty, this story should stop us in our tracks. This same God who did these things for Israel is the very same God that we in the West used to claim was our God, but now just like many Israelites said, we say he is irrelevant or non-existent.

HITTING A BRICK WALL - MAJOR EVENT 7

THE SEVENTH MAJOR EVENT

Now the point to this brief saga of ancient history and God, is that refusing to listen is decisively not a good idea but, instead, a very bad idea. God said, after their escape from Egypt, "When I've given you the land I promised to Abraham, don't forget me". He further said, "This is my set of rules, 10 Commandments - [1]This is who I am, and this is what I like." "If you don't forget me, you will be blessed – [2]If you do forget me, you will find just as I have saved you from Egypt and slavery, I'll let you become captive to surrounding nations, nations far worse than Egypt."

Was this warning heeded? [3]They certainly said God would be their God when he warned them at the Red Sea and they had just witnessed His awesome power that released them and freed them from their enemy, but then, preferring their own way instead, they soon forgot. No! They decided that their own way was best. A bit of God who delivered was good, but a little of other customs weren't bad either - trade with surrounding nations is excellent. Other nations' gods and their rituals have to be okay as well: a nice multi-cultural mix. The little "no", soon became a big "No Way!" [4]All warnings were treated with disdain or contempt. [5]Many sent to warn them were regarded as traitors to the national cause and we all know the fate of traitors.

So, have the Jews paid a price? Think about it. Persecuted relentlessly over thousands of years. (The couple of following references are just a sample of the Jewish rejection of God, then restoration back to their ancient Saviour and their homeland Israel) Evidence of mayhem on this race throughout the centuries - before B.C. to this day. Hitler's way of dealing with his little Jewish problem last century emphasizes this sad fact. He (Hitler) decided, rid the earth of every Jew. The only good Jew is a dead Jew. Find them all, kill them all. He almost succeeded, but not quite. Many today still regard Hitler with admiration, and as far as the Jews are concerned and in relation to his attitude towards them, would dearly love to follow in this tyrant's footsteps - its modern name is anti-Semitism (anti-Jew). This position is entrenched. For many nations in the Middle East, children throughout their education are trained to be anti-Semitic.

So how can such ancient stories, which are often hotly contested but never disproven, affect us or relate to us in any meaningful way in the 21st century. [6]God says, he is the same God now, as he was when he delivered the Jews from slavery in Egypt and gave them warnings concerning not listening and alternatively blessings if they would listen. We can learn more as each era unfolds but a common saying carries a noteworthy signal- "don't bite the hand that feeds you." - in this case especially the creator God who gave them their freedom, together with his instructions for successful living.

Of immense importance is the next major event. To grasp its significance to our planet, we need to go back in time: in fact, around 2000 years. Throughout the ancient world, but particularly in the history of Israel, [7]God has always promised a Messiah, a great king, a saviour who would deliver Israel from every oppressor. A great warrior, in the line of Israel's famous King David, who established the nation in the lead up to its glory days. Once again, in human terms an impossibility, but God has a plan beyond human capacity, and it will be completed to exact detail. Read on; you will see. It's a great prospect, but you will also see, as you read further, that to participate we need to listen and respond positively. In fact, in this regard, modern civilization will be seen to be little different from ancient races and, in many instances, even less likely to pay attention than the Israelites were.

GOOD NEWS ARRIVES - MAJOR EVENT 8

THE EIGHTH MAJOR EVENT

But how? As a BABY! God in the form of our humanity. Hey! That's just crazy. But no – God's idea, not ours; it's true. [1]He was born in Bethlehem, Israel – an event that was foretold around 650 years earlier. Then [2]his parents went hurriedly to Egypt – prophesied around 800 years beforehand, and after some time had elapsed, [3]they returned to Israel and Jesus' hometown Nazareth - also foretold around 700 years before the event. So how and why did this apparently unremarkable event occur the way it did? Unless we pay attention, we will miss the message, its significance, and its importance to our modern even seemingly enlightened lives.

[4]An angel visits Mary and tells her not to fear, because she has been chosen to bear God's son. The immediate troublesome thought to her is that being engaged to Joseph but not married would carry serious consequences. Expressing this natural alarm, the angel comforted her by saying that God would take care of this and that with him, nothing is impossible. This child was to be called Jesus. After this, Mary accepts and is convinced

and feels honoured, saying "I am the Lord's servant, let it be according to your word." Joseph is likewise worried and is given a clear, positive message from the angel, similar to Mary, and is at peace to marry her. The baby will be called the Son of God, also commonly known as Jesus of Nazareth. A Nazarene – the meaning of this word for a Jew – is 'despised'. This should carry a sobering thought - Jesus, Son of God, born in Bethlehem, coming out of Egypt, a Nazarene - DESPISED. So, what is this all about?

At the time of his birth, Rome ruled supremely and that included Israel. [5]Due to a Roman census, his parents had to travel to Bethlehem, Joseph's town of origin, to be counted. All accommodation was fully booked, so [6]a little space was set aside for mother, father, and baby out behind the Inn (hotel), with some animals - a rough start. At this time in a long line of conqueror's, Israel's latest conqueror, the Roman Empire, ruled almost all nations and exercised iron fisted control. It was a hard time for the Jews. [7]On hearing of this baby's arrival and its implications to his position, Jewish King Herod, appointed by Rome, tried to find and kill him, recklessly killing many babies in Bethlehem in the process. [8]His earthly parents escaped with baby Jesus to Egypt where they lived as fugitives for some years, until [9]the King who was looking for him died. They then returned to Nazareth, where Jesus was raised as the son of Joseph and Mary. Though a hunted fugitive, this unique child was not discovered, and he grew to manhood.

How could anything be good about this beastly Roman captivity for the Jews? Powerful nations are usually well practiced in the art of control, and Romans certainly had this art finely tuned. They kept their subjects in check, crushing all opposition but also giving favours to some key Jews. Although unbelievers themselves, they had built a beautiful temple in the heart of Jerusalem for the God of the conquered Jews. A fantastic temple, white marble, shining and huge, glistening from the horizon. For everyone entering Jerusalem, the message was, this must be where one can find God. They gave the Jewish religious leaders authority to rule Israelites across the land according to Jewish customs and traditions.

The only area where they did not allow Jewish control was the death penalty, which they reserved for themselves. Romans said: "All we want from our subjects is no rioting." "Remember, we are your masters, and as you are under Rome's protection, our tax law is universal. Rome does not directly collect tax; here in Israel indigenous Jews have this important work. For we Romans, it is all about money, our authority and peace."

Tax collectors were a major key to Rome's ongoing power. The indigenous tax collectors knew Roman law and made sure Rome got all they wanted. Tax collectors were paid from the money they solicited. What is our fee they would ask? Answer: anything you like, replied Rome. In the process of taking care of our needs look after your own interests. Whatever you charge, they will have to pay because, when you have the backing of the Empire, people know they have to do what they are told. Hated local tax collector Jews were called sinners and were an absolute anathema to their fellow Jews, but because they were under the full protection of Rome, they also became very rich.

This was the society into which Jesus Christ was born and raised. [10]At around 30 years of age and after [11]he was baptized and experienced temptation without fault, he began his earthly public work. They called him Rabbi, or Teacher, as he went from town to town across Israel and some surrounding non-Jewish areas. [12]Thousands followed him because he could readily heal all diseases, teach with unsurpassed authority, and perform outstanding miracles. He could also cast out demons including, can you believe, raising dead people to life. He riled the Jewish leaders in charge of the beautiful temple because of his unorthodox methods and the unusual ways he operated which were outside their society guidelines. For example, respected Rabbis at this time chose young key followers to train in their ways, and the most honoured Rabbis would select the best trainees from the most highly respected rabbinic schools. [13]Rabbi Jesus chose 12 such "insiders" as his key followers, but they were from the street – including untrained fishermen and even a hated tax collector. [14]When challenged, Jesus answered, I haven't come for righteous people, so called good people, but sinners for their repentance. Jewish religious leaders hated him and decided he had to be killed. They gave 3 main reasons:

1. He said he was God's son sent into the world from heaven, his usual place of abode from eternity past. [15]They knew him to be Mary and Joseph's son – the son of the Carpenter from Nazareth. A saying common to all Jews in that day was "nothing worth anything ever comes out of Nazareth." They agreed that he was a miracle worker, even accepting that he had raised dead people, but said all of it was done by evil power and not God's power. [16]This they said made him a liar and a blasphemer, which carried the death penalty.

2. He enraged Jewish leaders, calling them hypocrites and liars, as they turned part of the beautiful temple into a trading centre – exchanging money, selling animals for sacrifice, and charging extortionate temple tax. [17]He overturned their trade tables and drove them out with a whip saying, "this place is meant to be a place of prayer for all nations, but you have made it a den of thieves." [18]They said, "We are children of ancient Abraham." Jesus replied, "Well! If you were his children, you would welcome me as he did". They answered indignantly and in human terms, "you're not even fifty years old and yet you say you've seen Abraham"? He replied as only

God could "Before Abraham was – I AM". "I AM", was the term Jews reserved only for God. All they saw was a thirty-year-old upstart and they hated him for undermining their authority and believed his word to be blasphemous, which carried the death penalty. [19]He further replied: "No! Your father is the devil because you do his work. He was in the beginning a liar and murderer and so are you." [20]Jesus then turned to people and said: "These people (religious leaders) are blind guides without any truth; have nothing to do with them, they are wanting to kill me". Remember, these are the very ones in whom Rome had vested great power.

3. Jesus Christ, as we indicated, was raising dead people to life, with a particularly notable case, [21]Lazarus, just outside of Jerusalem. There were many witnesses, and common people were beginning to think in increasing number that he must be their long-promised king and deliverer – Israel's Messiah. These same religious leaders said, we don't dispute that he's raising the dead, but it's not by God's power, it's by the devil's power. [22]He must be killed, and [23]the dead he's raised must also be killed. This thing, they said, is getting out of hand. He is gaining ground and with so much power, we will lose ours, and Rome will not continue to help us. At last, they got their chance.

Every year for more than 1500 years, the Jews held a celebration they called Passover. It was to celebrate the time they were released from the slavery of Egypt, and it was a huge annual event. Though it was the ancient world to us, it was a little like Western Christmas celebrations, with foreigners coming to Jerusalem from all over the then known world. The city was packed and there were many unruly crowds. With everyone having noisy fun, it was the perfect time; no one would notice what was really going on. [24]One of Jesus' followers agreed to betray him for small money – 30 pieces of sliver. Following his arrest, with fake accusations and a mock trial [25](even Pilate, his Roman accuser said – I find him to be without fault), the Romans agreed to let him be crucified.

Now Jesus Christ, over his previous three years of work on earth was very clear; he said, "They will kill me; I have come from heaven as the true sacrifice for the sins of all mankind. No one can rightfully accuse me of sin as I have done no wrong and am without sin. My father has asked me, and I have agreed to be the sacrifice for the sins of all who will come and believe in me." Jesus further said, "No one takes my life from me; I have power to lay it down and power to take it up again. I have received this authority from my father." Yes! He said, [26]"Death has no hold on me. I will be put on the cross for the sins of the world and after three days, I will rise again." [27]"Just as by one man, sin came into the world and brought death, life is on offer now to all who believe in me – one man". [28]"People will have forgiveness of their sin through me and share in my life – One man God in flesh. I am the God of life, eternal life and all life. I have come to bring freedom from the power of sin (the going of mankind's own way) and death."

This is an outstanding claim with an equally outstanding promised gift, but is anyone listening? Well, yes and no. At his cross, Jesus Christ was not the only one to be crucified that day. Two others were nailed up also – one on his left, the other on his right. Through agony and a mocking crowd chanting, "Let's see how much this lunatic is God now!" "Let's see who, if anyone comes to save him; supposedly he saved others." "What? He can't even save himself!" [29]One of those crucified hurled the same abuse - "if you are God, get us off these crosses and get yourself off also." But the other said, [30]"Don't you respect God? Here we are dying for our offences, but this man has done no wrong." [31]Then he said, "Lord, remember me when you come in your kingdom!" Jesus replied, "and today you will be with me in Paradise."

So, who was listening? Certainly not the lost mocking crowd all parroting one another, nor the angry thief. They showed that all they wanted was God as they wanted him – one to answer immediate perceived needs or cravings. But he is and can only ever be the God who is. He is the God we all need, but not usually the God we want. However, yes! The repenting thief was listening, and in the midst of great trouble and excruciating pain he heard the word of forgiveness for his sins and the gift of eternal life. This thief made his decision to go for the God who is - the God of all power, comfort, and love. One thief is lost, the other, though dying, is saved.

God loves us all so much that he gives us this same Jesus, His only Son as his unique, perfect and exclusive gift, for the forgiveness of our sins and eternal life. This is a huge breakthrough, and no-one could have expected or seen it coming. It is a guaranteed true offer, but of our natural selves, because we find it beyond belief, we can easily miss it, refuse it, or pass it by.

Now, going forward, whoever believes in him will, like this listening thief, not be lost, but will also have forgiveness and eternal life. So, what is happening here? Both men are in the same situation, hopeless and helpless – dying. They both cry out, but their cries are vastly different. Is there something to consider here? Certainly, there is. There is a human principle on display, and it's shown clearly at the cross of Christ. There are two distinct lines of human thinking being revealed and they are found in every generation when once this message of the cross of Jesus Christ is known. But wait a minute, it is a 2000-year-old story. How is this relevant now?

It is totally relevant because, about God, many conclude that he says he can save us, but here is my judgement: If there is God, He would behave kindly and compassionately, as obviously there is a problem here – poverty, violence, inequality, injustice, starvation, war etc. If God is for real and can take remedial action, it's clearly reasonable that he should, and therefore would do something about all this. He does not, so he is not in any sense relevant, as far as I am concerned. This, in principle, is like the angry thief on the cross – if you can do something, God, then you should, so why don't you?

Alternatively, there is the response from the other thief. We can say, I am a person gone my own way and thought this to be okay. I have served my own self-interest and it's leading me the wrong way. So, Lord as you say, your death on Calvary's cross is for me; I am going to accept and agree with you. Because of your great love for me, I receive by faith your love. Please forgive me for going my own way as I now turn my life from this to you and your way. Now from the first emphatic demand, "fix the problem", heaven is silent. But from the second and far less often heard decision, [32]heaven lights up with forgiveness and eternal life and dances with joy. [33]The bridge across is accepting that I have a need and then accepting by faith the person of Jesus to answer it – both these are vital and work together. Jesus is the Son of God, and maker/sustainer of all life. The gift is on offer, but will it be received or rejected?

When he died on that cross, it was out of love for me, an undeserving sinner, so that I can be forgiven and have his gift, eternal life. I will agree with what God says; [34]all have sinned and come short of his standard. Further, I am going to believe God when he says that [35]without the shedding of blood, there is no remission for sin. Jesus was made sin for me and shed his blood so that now, through my believing in Him, I can be reconciled to my Father God. To further emphasize, this is why

[36]Jesus cried out on that cross, "my God, my God, why have you forsaken me?" It was because on his cross though a perfect human being, he carried the weight of my sin. Having cried this, Jesus loudly said: [37]"It is finished!", then he died.

This is consistent throughout the record during his life on earth. When anyone asked Him what is most important for mankind whilst living, he would reply: To believe God and to believe in the one whom he had sent. [38]In his recorded prayer he says, "Father, this is eternal life that they believe in you, the one true God and Jesus Christ whom you have sent". His work in this world is to save us through breaking sin's power, brought about through the exercise of our own way, and give us eternal life in its place.

[39]Jesus Christ says: "Be sure to enter heaven by the narrow gate. The gate is wide and the road is broad that leads to destruction (eternal separation from God) and many go that way. The gate is narrow and the road also is narrow that leads to life (eternal life with God) and only a few find it. History will show that majority opinions are often wrong – in the case of God and his Son Jesus Christ, totally wrong. Jesus tells us to make sure we do not go with the widely held belief of those on this broad road, as it leads to an eternity separated from our maker God. God is saying to everyone instead, be wise and come to me through my Son.

Unlike the previous time when no one listened at the flood except one person and his family, since Jesus Christ came, though few seem to listen and take action by believing in him through faith or trust, the number is continuing to grow and across the generations, probably even now the number of people is beyond counting. [40]This bears out the word of Jesus Christ when he says, "My name will be known from shore to shore as waters cover the sea".

Although comparatively speaking only a few from each generation accept Jesus, collectively from all the generations it represents a huge number. Nevertheless, with such a wonderful gift on offer – eternal life - why is it that so few believe? This next event should not seem outlandish or impossible. After all, it was clear even to His enemies that he had miracle working power, but to them, any raising of the dead he performed was through evil power and not God. Here, we need to carefully consider,[41] Jesus answered to the challenge regarding His use of evil power in the following way. [42] "If the devil casts out the devil, his power is finished. If I cast him out by God's power, then his power is broken, and God's kingdom is breaking in and coming to you." But what about dying and rising to life again? He always said he would, but again, it's crazy talk – no-one believed this was for real. Wasn't the thief on the cross just grasping at straws?

If the resurrection is true, then all history pivots on it, and all the future is to be governed by it. If it isn't, he and all his witnesses, including this one, are deluded, cheats or liars. However, if true, the case is that not one iota of so-called cancel culture either in society or with an individual will make a shred of difference to God's universal plan.

THE INTERNATIONAL GAME CHANGER - MAJOR EVENT 9

THE NINTH MAJOR EVENT

He, Jesus Christ, is leaving this World as the Son of God with all Power and Authority[1]. Now remember, Jesus said to the thief who accepted him at Calvary: "Today you will be with me in Paradise". Jesus also says on many occasions that he had come here to die for our sins – a seemingly senseless death indeed but illustrated by the following picture: In the court is a judge, in the dock is the accused. The accused is well aware of his impossible financial debt. The judge, upholder of justice, passes sentence. Then, to everyone's amazement, the judge steps down from his bench and says to the jury, I will pay the debt for this person.

In a small picture like this, we see something of God's burning love for what he knows is his lost creation. He sets the penalty, then out of pure love, pays the highest price on his cross at Calvary, to cover the worst to the smallest sin. Any offence puts a barrier between God and humanity because he cannot deny his own holiness; with God there is no fault, no wrong thought, no wrong deed. [2]His remedy for us is called God's folly, but then he says His foolishness is wiser than we are.

Now this same Jesus who kept his eye on target so we could have the benefit of sins forgiven and eternal life, made yet another statement which, at the time, made absolutely no sense. Usually, when forecasting his death, he would say: [3]"But after three days, I will rise from the grave. You will see. Then you will believe that I am the one who conquers death and am above all. Yes! You will see me again – after three days." Now when his friends heard him, they certainly were not listening; they did not want to hear and couldn't understand. [4]Instead, they reckoned "our leader must be completely sleep deprived, unhinged, deranged, hallucinating – he needs a rest. His behaviour is highly suspect and anything but normal. [5]Resurrection – no way! It's silly talk. In his right mind, he wouldn't say anything like this and certainly he'll never follow through with it." [6]But he did, and his self- proclaimed, rock-solid friends all just ran away in fear and hid themselves.

A great deal was happening when he died and on that day the sun went dark at 3pm. It was terrifying for his followers but the religious leaders were happy because at last they had their man! They could finally put an end to the previous three years of dangerous nonsense and society could return to normal once again. A fitting end to the fake Messiah rubbish they'd been dealing with for years. [7]Then a rich person came forward and went to the authorities with a once sceptical religious leader and requested his body saying, "He can be buried in the tomb I've made for myself". This sounded good, "dead and buried". The religious leaders made their point saying, "While living, this blasphemer said he would, after three days, come back to life. [8]So, to stop any wild rumours spreading, could we make the grave secure and place a guard there? No worries, said the Romans, seal it to make it secure and we will supply guards, good as done. [9]

However, at the appointed time (three days) in addition to a number of cosmic events - there was an earthquake. Frightened soldiers ran off or fell down in fear and the stone seal was rolled away from Jesus' tomb. Exactly as he had already said, after three days, Jesus started showing himself to his followers and many other people as well. Some saw the grave seal removed, no soldiers around and went inside. They saw his grave clothes, but though they went with ointment to embalm him, Jesus' body was not there.[10] Amazed, they were met instead by two beings from the place from which Jesus always said he had come from to Earth. [11]These angels said: "Why are you looking for the living among the dead. He is not here but risen, just as he told you." "Now go to Lake Galilee, you will see him there. [12]Also, before he died, he told you that's where you will meet him." Whenever people saw him for the first time, his usual greeting was: "Don't be afraid, it is I, touch me and see – A ghost doesn't have flesh and bones like me". [13]At one point, 500 people who were gathered in one place saw him. [14]Also in another recorded instance, he chastised a couple for their inability to grasp the truth and significance of his resurrection.

Then, we have the most commonly quoted, doubting Thomas, who was somewhere else when all the ten friends of Jesus originally saw him. [15]They told Thomas but he said, "Unless I personally can see his wounds and touch them, I will never believe." When the risen Jesus finally caught up with Thomas, he said, "Now Thomas, I've heard about you. Have your way – put your hand into my side and your fingers into my wounds – stop being faithless and believe!" Bowing down, Thomas replied, "My Lord and my God!" Jesus said to him, "Now as you've seen me you believe- the same blessing you have just now received through seeing me, will rest on all who won't see me, and yet believe".

Could we not stop here and think? Our common saying "seeing is believing" will not work in this instance, however because of Thomas' insistence of being answered with 100% assurance on his part, then anyone who claims this crucified and risen Lord Jesus Christ as their own Lord and God will receive the same blessing as this hardened sceptic. As you read further, you will see how this blessing is both personal and all surpassing.

After this and many other sightings, Jesus said, "My work on earth is completed. [16]I am going back - to where I came from - [17]to my Father and your Father, to my God and your God." [18]"Do not worry, my leaving here is better for you. [19]I've taught you, and after some days, I'll send my Spirit." "This same Spirit that raised me from the dead, he (my presence) will be with you and in you forever." [20]"From this time also, all who believe in me will receive the gift of this same Spirit – my Spirit. To have my Spirit is life – eternal life. When people hear of my love through your witness, I will personally back up what you say by my Spirit, so do not fear. My Spirit will also call people to myself. When they come to me, I will forgive their sins, reconcile them to my Father and myself through my death and my life." "Through the gift of my Spirit, to those who believe, I will empower them to live for God rather than themselves and I will give them the gift of eternal life. There will be strong opposition, but don't be afraid, I have overcome all and through me, you will also." [21]"So confidently go into all the world with the message of my love and I will be with you always, in every generation." He left those friends and returned to the place from where he had been sent to the earth and [22]His followers willingly decided to take his wise advice, telling everyone he was risen from the dead.

[23]Meanwhile, the lying religious leaders paid money to the guards who had lost their man saying: "Tell the people that his followers somehow stole his body while we were on 'sleeping duty' and if anyone says anything to us, we will back up your story." Regardless, Jesus' enthusiastic followers went to Jerusalem and [24]early in the morning while they were together praying, a huge rushing wind came, [25]tongues of fire fell on the believers, and [26]to the large multicultural, multilingual crowds from all parts of the then known world, just as Jesus had said, people started to hear the resurrection message in their own language. It's a miracle, but no problem for God – He had done this already, thousands of years before, to send people on their way across the earth, but this time, it was to bring people together to believe in Him. Many were impressed to say the least! [27]The usual scoffers called out, don't listen! They are early morning drinkers – drunks. [28]One of the new believers, now gifted in speech, explained what was happening and thousands believed then and there, as they received the promised Spirit by faith. [29]They showed love and kindness and moved from their past futile ways of superstitions, greed, and revenge as they yielded to the love of God. For them, they had been made new, just as Jesus Christ had said would happen. People everywhere were amazed and gave the credit to God, honouring the creator.

[30]Everyone was happy, except the religious leaders, who were incensed that all [31]their efforts were failing to stop this 'fake Messiah' whom they had only just killed. [32]They began chasing down believers, putting them on trial, killing some, with some having miraculous escapes. This sorry saga, as well as for the Jews, has continued in varying parts of the world across the centuries until this day, again just as Jesus said it would. Jesus calls himself the head of his church, and believers in him, his body. Further, he says that when his body is complete (never a date given), he will return for all who believe in him, and the

present world order will finish. He says he will continue to build this body of believers and though many attempted efforts have and will continue to be made to shut it down, these have not and will never succeed. Light overcomes darkness and love overcomes hate.

11

THE ULTIMATE VICTORY - MAJOR
EVENT 10

THE TENTH MAJOR EVENT

Jesus' purpose now is to take back the world he has made and have his body of believers with him[1]. He says very clearly, just as I go away, I will return and make all of this happen at the right time. [2]So, the question asked by his friends quite naturally was, when are you going to do all this? He replied, "This timing is with my Father, and it is not for you." As with everything relating to God, though people are warned to look out for this, because they are disbelieving, they don't. It will be a global and unmissable event; every mouth (sceptics, doubters, and unbelievers) will be stopped when he returns. It could be closer than we all think. At this point some readers may want to press the exit button and "get off the bus" because, in human terms, it sounds incredible. However, it is of utmost importance to stay with the narrative. In his day on Earth, no one denied that Jesus raised dead people, the evidence stared them in the face. However, confronted with this power his enemies wanted to kill him. They decided to say that although he did obvious miracles, it was done by an evil power, not God's power.

They knew he had said he would rise again, so they planned to block this also. However, with every attempt ever made to prevent God from doing what he had decided, it failed. Resurrection is a specialty reserved for the power of God. We should not think it's strange. With God, the God of life, nothing is impossible. Of equal importance in the days of Jesus' life on earth, evidence of his resurrection was so clearly seen and recorded, that the only answer his enemies could mount was the spreading of lies as widely and as quickly as possible. They even paid large sums of money in order to establish these false explanations. We should not be surprised. It is human nature on display, which springs into action whenever a narrative other than the reality is desired. For Jesus' resurrection and the surrounding miraculous occurrences, this was seen as the necessity.

We need to get this, but of ourselves we don't, and we can't. We need serious help – help we may never have previously considered. You will see how this writer received the needed help. Darkness may be real, but so is light. So, take heart, light is stronger.

Very few are listening! There are signs of the last days everywhere! It is wisdom we need to be listening to. Jesus Christ has already warned about this saying, [3]"be sure to keep watch". We should consider that all the important previous signs have never been taken seriously by the majority and yet all have been Earth changing events, fulfilled exactly as foretold. [4]Jesus says that not one word of all that has been said, will remain unfulfilled. This is worth noting also, "not one word".

Jesus Christ, when illustrating his return in the form of stories, made the point, "When I return, will anyone be listening, will anyone be watching for this!" This should concern everyone, because who is listening now? A long time before Jesus' birth, his death, his resurrection and his return were being foretold, all but a very few, recognised it. No one understood God's word for what it was and is.

Example A: Isaiah the prophet, around 2600 years ago speaking of Jesus, writes: [5]"Who has believed our message" – Jesus comes. He was despised and rejected. He was pierced for our wrongdoing, the Lord (God Almighty) put our punishment on Himself because we all have gone our own way; we all turned our back on God's way, and we are dead to God and cannot save ourselves. He was killed for our wrongs. Though there was no violence or deceit in Him. He was buried in a rich man's tomb, but it was God's plan. Though He died, he will rise and never die again – and with all power and authority (Jesus' resurrection). He has made the way to eternal life for us and more. He is calling those who will believe this message, the strong and the great.

The question posed is, will we be counted among the relative few who believe and participate in Jesus' victory at calvary. Will we accept His gift of forgiveness of sins and friendship with God our maker and the gift of his Spirit of peace? Alternatively, will we decide to stay with unbelief and scepticism, joining the mockers and scoffers who appear now to be the great and the strong. The eternal word is: [6]Whoever has the Son of God has life. Whoever does not have the Son of God, does not have life.

As is seen, God has a tremendous future for those who love, believe, and trust Him. Accepting God's love, we enter Heaven. Staying with our own way, we cannot go there. No amount of money or good deeds now will suffice, only Jesus' finished work, culminating in His resurrection and our acceptance of it, and him as our sure help, is the road that leads to Heaven.

Example B: Isaiah also prophesied, [7]"Unto us, a child is born, unto us, a son is given." The government will be on his shoulders. His name will be called "Wonderful, Counsellor, the Almighty God, the Everlasting Father, the Prince of Peace, and of his name, and the increase of his government – there will be no end." This refers to Jesus Christ and was foretold around 2650 years ago. The meaning of the name Jesus – "the Lord saves" – [8]He will save his people from their sins. The meaning of the name Christ – "the anointed one". When these two words are joined, they mean Jesus Christ: God's appointed judge and ruler of the world. God is continuing to move toward this climactic implementation, and nothing will, in the finish, prevent this from happening.

Example C: This prophet, King David, 3000 years ago goes straight to the death of Jesus Christ on the cross and says: [9]"My God, My God! Why have you forsaken me? I am scorned, despised, mocked and insulted." Then he says: [10]"I am poured out like water. My heart is turned to wax, and all my bones are out of joint, and you lay me in the dust of death." To explain, this grotesque description is because this is what happens when a living body is hung on a cross. Who knew to write in such a way? This writer spoke 800 years before the cross punishment was invented by the Romans of Jesus' day. But then just as amazing, is what follows by this same writer. [11]He says: "There is a remarkable victory. Everyone who looks to God will live forever. [12]Everyone will acknowledge this one, kneeling and bowing before this king. Future generations will be told about Him and say: [13]He has done it!". Done what, we may well ask? The ancient prophet in a detailed and accurate account written hundreds of years prior to the fulfilment of this event then says: "Their hearts will live forever". So here is the consistent picture. Jesus' coming, his death, his resurrection, and his gift of eternal life for those who trust Him. How could such accounts as these be given and many more? If you listen to the word of sceptics, they say that someone must have found the way to insert the history of these so called 'Prophecies' after the event and then made them look like a future word – but this just doesn't make sense. Will we foolishly believe a false theory such as this with no proof because we prefer it or, accept the truth of what God's says. [14]God has a word for us. He says, "People can only tell you what they think might have happened." "Listen to me and you will understand what has occurred and what is going to take place in the future." [15]God further says, "I not only know the end from the beginning, but I am also the beginning and the end." [16]"I am God and no one else is, look to me and you will be saved." Who but God could give such an exact description? This is just one of many accounts, written at different times in history about the coming and future of his son 1000 years before it happened? We should note this because it's as relevant for us 3000 years later as it was when it was first written. Bearing in mind that these early writers could not have known the future time they were writing about, or the prevailing world conditions of our present experience, the message they brought is arguably even more relevant for us today than it was for them. However, for many, all of life's goals and possessions are seemingly within reach and for some, already attained. When considered alongside the word of Jesus Christ, many may think, why should I bother with God? I have all I need already. [17]No, says God, this view is short-sighted and empty! [18]What is the point of gaining the whole world yet forfeit your life? What can you give in exchange for this?

You see, God is saying that this life he brings us into is like a shadow. It appears for a short time but soon vanishes. He then says it (life) is like a building which to last needs a solid foundation and a quality builder. God says the relationship between solid foundation and quality building is vital. God then tells us that the solid foundation for our life is Jesus Christ, His Son and the master builder is our Father God, both our maker and sustainer. Left to our own devices, we end up with our building on the sand – not capable of withstanding the storms of life. Likewise, our building if on sand, beautiful though it may outwardly appear, cannot remain for long and cannot last.

I. **Prophecy of Jesus** - When Jesus came, people asked him, "You say you have come here but will leave and then come back here again. [19]How will we know, when and where you will come, what should we look for? Will there be any signs?" [20]Jesus replied, "There will be, though you need to be on guard because many will speak appealing, but false words that lead people astray. Those who look to God will be able to understand. For several examples, [21]There will be times of stress with [22]people being very fearful. Just look, billions of dollars are now being spent each year for mental illness caused by stress in every nation. This continues to increase with no end in sight. [23]People will be lovers of pleasure rather than lovers of God, which is self-evident. [24]Nation will rise against nation. Wars and rumours of war with many refugees. [25]Famines in various places and [26]earthquakes. [27]An increase in knowledge, but without God. No-one would argue with any of this, and Jesus squarely puts it to us in these few signs and many others not mentioned here, that when these in combination are taking place, you may know God is true to His word of returning and establishing the kingdom referred to previously in vision and story form. Importantly, [28]this message of God's love for his world is to be offered to all nations. Jesus says: [29]"Heaven and earth will pass away, but my word will not pass away."

2. **Prophecy of Jesus** - As already mentioned, in the last days there are many other signs, but significantly, against all human predictions, the Jews, after almost 2000 years of being scattered across the earth, have once again returned as a nation to Israel.

When Jesus was taken away to be crucified, he said: [30]"Don't cry for me, cry for yourselves and your children, [31]now your land (place of living) has been left desolate and you will be scattered." True to what He said, in AD70, just 30 years after Jesus was crucified, the Romans became so infuriated with the Jews, after killing thousands they said: "Leave Israel, just go and never come back!" History calls this "The Dispersion". Jews said, "Where will we go?" Romans replied: "We don't care, just leave," and so they left their land and became stateless, taking up residence wherever they could. This has been their position for the last 2000 years. So why are they back in their land now? How did this happen? It came about because of the Holocaust. After World War II and the attempted Jewish extermination by Hitler, many nations were aghast and said, this endless killing of Jews must stop, but how? They are killed and mercilessly persecuted because they have no land of their own. The solution: A vote by an international committee was taken and through an extremely narrow margin, the Jews were given back some of the land of Israel and reclaimed more of it in a short war with Egypt in 1967. The fact that nations could meet together and take such a decision, is a further sign which Jesus said would be a mark of the last days.

3. Prophecy of Jesus - [32]Speaking through his apostle John in prison on the Island of Patmos, Jesus indicated that - the clamour for world government will become stronger and stronger until eventually everyone will accept it. We could call it in our world today, the global response to a global challenge, in a global village – the pressure is relentless but, it appears to make good sense. [33]According to Jesus Christ, in the beginning, this world government will look very good and will seem to achieve excellent results, especially in the field of resolving international conflicts. [34]However, in the end, without God, it turns out to be horrific. He said, "We show that we are sure we can go better without God, but the result shows we can't." [35]"Unless I return, and the time of world violence and chaos is shortened, no flesh would survive." He likened these days to conditions which were in place just before the great flood in the days of Noah – outlining the very way of the world we live in now. This being the case, Jesus Christ could return at any time.

[36]Even in the midst of those days, God says: "I will hold out my love to anyone who will accept me and save them eternally, but [37]he warned that most get angrier – cursing God, mocking God, and refusing to come to God." "They refuse to accept my love through Jesus, my son, who died for sins, and insist that only their own way is worth choosing." God is loving beyond our imagination and, for each of us individually, he has our best interests at heart for this life and he says we can fully trust him for the next as well. He is saying that when we go our own way, very serious consequences with fixed outcomes lie ahead and He doesn't want this for anyone. He is going to visibly overcome His enemy and wants us to share in His victory. He wants us, through the new life Jesus alone can give, to side with him and experience His ultimate victory – the total abolition of sin and death, which he has already guaranteed by his own resurrection when he came here, some 2000 years ago.

4. Prophecy of Jesus - Jesus again says, [38]"They will not believe even if someone rises from the dead to tell them because, if they will not believe what is written, they will not believe what is spoken either." It is written in the Word of truth, [39]"In the last days, people will be learning and learning, listening to anybody, but never coming to learn the truth". He further says, [40]"Therefore, because they will turn from truth, instead, they will wander off into myths" (A myth is any interesting story, which is not true). This is precisely what many people are doing already, and God has said, [41]"when they do, remember I have already told you that they will". He said, [42]"So be ready, because if you are not, you will find I will return when you do not expect, and you will not be able to come with me. [43]Alternatively, if you die before I come and have not chosen me, you will die with your way and not mine. Where I am, you will not be able to come. [44]I love you; I am love. I made you, I am the life and I want you and me to enjoy life in abundance. This is the way God always intended for His creation before sin came into the world. [45]In my view (God's), this "sin" has caused a temporary problem – not necessarily permanent. Therefore, wouldn't it be wise to not decide against God and His love? Why would anyone continue to reject God and turn what he says is a temporary problem into a permanent one? [46]Now is the best time to repent and this means, turn from my way to God's way. Accept Jesus as Saviour and Lord because that is who He is. God is showing that He loves us, and when we turn to him, He will forgive our waywardness and give us His gift of new life. He says,[47] [48]If anyone comes to me; I never send them away. I will receive them and make them new. [49]For all who come this way, the old life has gone for them – finished - the new life has come. It is all about not rejecting Jesus but accepting him." What a beautiful offer – forgiveness, life and a future as certain as His resurrection! The final word of the risen Jesus is: be ready because regardless of what anyone says or thinks, [50]I am coming soon.

12

TESTIMONY – LIGHT IN THE DARKNESS

As I have written of these events, it is reasonable for you to query, *"How can one have confidence that this writer knows what he is talking about?"* I am a 77-year-old man, married to a beautiful wife this last 55 years with two children and five grandchildren. I was raised and educated in a loving family in western civilization in Australia. As a teenager, I decided the Christian message was not for me, that it was not going to have any influence or bearing on my settled way of life. I could say I was Christian, but there were many appealing choices and by late teens with a stable economic and social base, I was happy with good friends and future prospects were looking excellent. I was not thought of as a bad person and enjoyed sports and outdoor activities. Having tried my family's Christian ways, my considered opinion was that it wasn't for me; they could have their way, I had mine.

Before reading further, I mention that what I am telling you now, is difficult to describe, because the world according to me was about to be completely shattered. The thoughts in my mind at the time were - finish work, get early tea, go to college etc. and this positioned me in such a way that I had no idea of what was about to happen.

Weeks earlier, on an interstate holiday, I heard someone say, "I thought, I was a Christian, but discovered, that I wasn't." At that time, the comment was meaningless to me and, like many things we hear, we forget quickly we even heard them. The holiday finished, my work and friends inspired me, all was going well, recent pleasant memories were comforting but fading. However, after lunch break on this particular day, the plans for the evening ahead were suddenly interrupted. A deep inner conviction cut through my focus and challenged me. "Remember that comment you heard on your holiday?" I had forgotten, but clear as crystal it came back to me. "That message you heard, is a picture of your life also." "Like that person, you think you are fine – even Christian, but no, you are not. In fact, you are in a dark place, the place of the lost".

Believing I was not a bad person and considering many to be worse than me, I argued dismissively with this for several hours, until the workday was near finishing at 5pm. It was to no avail; nothing I raised by way of being a good person etc. made any difference. The description of my life returned with the same urgency - unless you change you will have no future and be separated from your Creator for all time.

Frustration was building. I had no desire to continue these unsettling thoughts, however as their persistence only increased, I began to realise that this must be a serious matter – worthy of my attention. For the first time in my life, I felt exposed, lacking for an answer, as the true picture of my life was starting to make an impact. Though work was finishing for the day, and I was preparing for college, this disturbing issue took priority. All I could think of now was to leave work, sit alone and ask God to show me what I needed to do. I had some background knowledge of things one could do.

1. [1]Believe that Jesus died for my sins. I knew I had done some wrong things but I hadn't felt I was all that bad, so I tried to think about that. Do you know, when I really gave it thought, I knew I did not believe in Jesus this way and never had, although now I felt I needed to. Did Jesus Christ really die for my sins? I could not, of myself, believe something like this – it just wasn't in my head space.

2. I had heard that [2]faith in God (trust) was needed, and I also gave this some thought. Again, I knew that I did not have any – certainly not in this way. I had faith in myself and in my capacity as an achiever. Never before had I experienced a power so strong, steady and totally grounded, messaging me until I was worn out. The one point only was, that unless I radically changed, I was in a dark place, lost, and heading towards it. This was me! No belief in Jesus Christ, no faith to trust in God. I did not have any and could not achieve it myself.

As I considered this, I realized the message had made its mark on my inner being. As if knowing I was committed to addressing the issue, all became silent. I felt alone, knowing that I had a deep need - Jesus died for sins, and required faith in Him. So, I decided, if these two pointers were true and outside of my capacity, [3]I would ask God to grant them and would remain seated until belief and faith became my reality. Time passed. You could call it "the agony of a lost soul" in a state of transition spanning an afternoon and evening. The night had fallen, and I was tired with seemingly no response. I thought any hope of an answer was disappearing.

On lifting my eyes, there before me was a vision of the cross. Suddenly, I received clarity that God in His love had allowed His Son, Jesus Christ to die for my sins and take them away. I could trust Him for this and put my faith in the living God. I did not wait to be told, I could leave that seat, I knew the gift was given. I went on air down the street, not being able to comprehend that the weight of guilt I had been carrying through determinedly living my own way had, in an instant, been removed. I had never realized the prison I had been in had weighed down so heavily on me and now I was free. I know what it means in this life to be a sinner (going my own way) and then – a sinner saved by God's Grace (accepting God's way.) It is what God means when he says: [4]"If anyone is in Christ, they are a new creation – the old is gone, the new is come."

Through this newfound gift of faith and belief in God, I knew I had been made NEW. This was of course, many years ago. I was 17 years of age then, however at the time of publishing this book in 2021 I was 77. Of one thing I am sure; God is real, is true, only does good, and can be relied on as a faithful friend 100%. Though unaware at the time, the experience I went through that day was the power of God's Spirit - this beautiful and truthful Spirit who came into the world, when Jesus left it. [5]Jesus said: "In my absence, I will send my Spirit, the Spirit of truth. He convicts the world (me and all who will listen and look for God) of sin (because they don't believe in me) of what is right (because my Father sent me, and I am returning to Him) and of judgement (because judgement is a certainty and the place of the lost is a real place). [6]My enemy (the devil), says Jesus, thought he could defeat me, but he is losing his grip. [7]I love my children – my creation. To pay for their sin has not been easy but it was worth it. The Devil reckoned they would not believe, but many have and will now continue to share fully in my victory. This has been my lived experience since coming to Christian faith. My conviction that this is the truth, if anything, grows stronger with the passing of time.

Does this mean I am now perfect and therefore everything in life works out accordingly? OR, does it mean that if I do wrong, it doesn't matter because God has forgiven my sins? A HUGE 'no way!' I am far from perfect and often have failed. What it does mean, is that in every circumstance, fair weather or stormy, God works for the good. It isn't fate, good luck, or anything like that. No! [8]Nothing can separate me or anyone whose trust is in God through Jesus Christ from His love. [9]There is forgiveness with God, so that we may learn what it is to have awesome respect for Him. God's forgiveness is complete and has put my life in a safe and secure position with Him. Though not conversant with much detail at the time, that day was incredibly significant because when I asked God to save me, I was asking Him into my life, and He is the Lord. Learning to treat Him that way, with our natural mentality being 'me first', is a lifetime journey. I now don't need to deny the truth and self-justify, there are no more disappointments with the endless broken New Year resolutions. Instead, I can ask for and receive strength to turn from my mistakes – no more excuses like "oh well, tough but I'm only human." This is true victory over sin. [10]I have learnt that Jesus loves me and that those who trust him are his children. He calls us His children. [11]He tells us He found us like lost sheep. [12]He keeps us safe and gives eternal life to those who trust Him. [13]God, and only God, has the power to forgive sins and claim us as His own, now, and forever.

Very interesting, some might say, and yet again others, why did I waste my time to read this madness? Or perhaps, as far as this writer's testimony is concerned, people have their thoughts, and they vary greatly. He says a word clear as crystal cut through. Maybe he had inner concerns in the subconscious and needed therapy. I can see that's his belief; good for him.

Mine is different, but mine is good for me; I'll go with the saying; to each his own.

Against these suppositions, [14]in the Word of Truth, we are told:

1. God's word is living and active.
2. It's sharper than any two-edged sword.
3. It penetrates, even dividing soul and spirit, joints and marrow.
4. It judges thoughts and attitudes of the heart (our centre of being).
5. It's discerning – giving insight to our thoughts and intentions.
6. Hidden – nothing is hidden from God's sight, all is totally transparent.
7. Giving account – everything is absolutely clear with God before whom we all must give account.

These seven points from the Word of Truth, align with the writer's experience and have nothing and never have had anything to do with a confused person in need of therapy.

13

FACT OR FICTION

With all of God's love on offer, why is there any problem? Humanly, we even say - genuine love is stronger than death. We have examples: Soldiers will die for their country and their mates; close friends will go into danger rather than see their friends in trouble. However, with us and God, it is very different. He is speaking, but so are we. Let's go back to the beginning and the 10 events in time that no one saw coming and why. Shouldn't we look at these and consider our own disposition, in the light of what God says and our response?

A GREAT START (Major Event 1)

We say – God is not the maker and he didn't make me, I am self-made. I have evolved and am evolving with continued improvements.

[1]**God the Maker says** – I am Creator, and I made all, but they (my created people) decide to go their own way.

CATASTROPHIC END: THE FLOOD (Major Event 2)

We say – We say this story of the flood and Noah is a myth. I am going to say there was a lot of water (inland seas) and based on the science, these seas gradually receded. We have scientific evidence. So, I am going to stay with the educated position on this one. It makes far more sense than an uneducated myth.

[2]**Creator God says** – Mankind's heart is totally depraved and hardened against me. There is incessant violence. We will have to start again. Only one person (him and his family respects me.)

UNFINISHED PROJECT (Major Event 3)

We say – Language change has happened and will always occur over time. It is only natural, and it is still going on. No God needed for this. Anyone would have to leave their brains elsewhere to believe this patchy story about "The Tower of Babel" and sudden language change.

[3]**The Word of Life says** – I have told humans they can now populate the earth I've made for them. The flood is over, and life is normalized; it's a brand-new start. But they only want to stick to one place, band together and make a big name for themselves. We will change their language, and this pride-inducing project they envisage will not further proceed.

PEOPLE ON THE MOVE (Major Event 4)

We say – Primitive man was unscientific, so naturally they worshipped nature, sun god, moon god, blocks of wood and stone etc. They had to defend themselves with clubs and spears etc. It has nothing to do with man's way vs. God's way. Everything is moving forward in an evolutionary upward pattern – no God but no problem.

⁴**God says** – I have made it happen. People are now able to spread across the Earth, but unfortunately, they are back to their old ways – making gods for themselves. Nevertheless, if they choose, they can still come to me. Earth demonstrates my handiwork, as the infinite being; the heavens absolutely speak my glory.

INTERNATIONAL CONNECTION (Major Event 5)

We say – The origin of the Jewish race is a great story but like all ancient stories, it contains some myth, legend, and exaggeration, which makes it fiction. Like all ancient stories or fictions, it has elements of truth, even some worthwhile ideals, but literal truth? No! Unbelievable.

⁵**God says** – A change is due. I am going to call a person from an idol worshipping family and community. This person trusts in me. With one person, I will make my name known strongly to him and his descendants. Ultimately, through one of his offspring my saving power is going to be made known and available to all people on Earth.

SLAVERY TO FREEDOM (Major Event 6)

We say – All this about Father Abraham is a huge and epic story, anyone with expertise could make it into a great movie, even a blockbuster, as some have. Show me some history on this, and I might believe it. Though Egypt did not record her defeats, there is doubt cast about this very ancient story and, besides, many nations went through large shifts in population, so why not in this case also?

[6]**God says** – It's time for the Jews to leave Egypt. They are being crushed in their slavery. I have chosen the man, Moses, who at the age of 80, will after these 450 years in Egypt, take them into the land I promised their forefather, Abraham.

HITTING A BRICK WALL (Major Event 7)

We say – What on earth could God, if he is genuine, have been thinking of? The Jews traded with surrounding nations – everyone did this. Those nations were very powerful, so in sharing their trade, how could they not share customs also? Why is God so exclusive? If he is for real, he must at least, be eccentric, certainly very strange.

[7]**God says** – Trying to talk to these people is just like talking to a brick wall. Now that I have delivered them, they should always respect me. [8]They could show to other nations my love, power and protection, then others would be impressed with me. [9]Instead, they are starting to follow the gods of the nations, instead of me. Why would they do this? Why no loyalty?

GOOD NEWS ARRIVES (Major Event 8)

We say – This 2000-year-old mystic called Jesus arrived, saying he is the one sent from God. Many have said this of themselves before he came, and also since – so many theories, no one can know for sure. This Jesus story full of differing interpretations, even to the point of sometimes causing wars. He obviously was a good man, but Son of God? No, I think that is going too far.

[10]**God says** – My people the (Jews) haven't been listening to me through my servants. Now is the right time. I will send my Son. [11]He will come in human form as a baby. [12]He will do everything exactly as we've agreed; our love calls for it. He will walk in my way and just as always, he will be perfect. The relationship problem between my creation and me is their sin. [13]Just like sheep go astray and wander off and get lost, so my people wander away from me, going their own way. My Son will pay the price for their sins. I love my creation and people. Through my Son I will forgive them, and for those who will accept my love, all will be made right.

THE INTERNATIONAL GAME CHANGER (Major Event 9)

We say – Jesus who grew to manhood and fell out with authorities is an intriguing story, but it did not fit in with ancient culture, and it does not fit in with ours either. To suggest that somebody who died has come to life again is unbelievable. Eternal life? Nobody knows for sure! No one knows if there is life after death. Good people may go to Heaven, and bad people elsewhere - I am willing to take my chances. When I really think about it, it sounds like so much nonsense. It is hard to think how anybody could believe this. A more accurate saying would have to be – pie in the sky when you die.

[14]**God says** – Now that my Son is risen from death, mankind is freely forgiven from their sins. The work is done- finished. [15]My Son now has all power and authority, so to all who believe in Him he will also give eternal life and we will share this life forever. [16]They will be called "my children" and ultimately there will be no more dying, just as I originally planned. [17]My people who already believe, will go and share this **good news** across the world to all generations.

THE ULTIMATE VICTORY (Major Event 10)

We say – History records that 2000 years ago Jesus came, but he has never been seen since, and if he was really coming again, he would surely be here by now. This "gospel" or "good news" as it is called is nothing more than plain foolishness for all to see. What does it achieve? Nothing! and if that's not all, it deludes people with false hope. For the economy, it does nothing. Even worse, children are taught this rubbish, and something will have to be done to protect them from this damaging type of impractical education. It does not even agree with science, which has improved the lives of countless people. It is not we who are deluded, deceived - It is those people who believe this line of fakery. Everything of the same previous so called nine epochs, are far more reasonably explained as natural events. As far as God's accepting people or not, we all know in this world there are good people and bad people. Generally speaking, people do the best they can, so if there is God, any fair God, he would accept them. As far as we are concerned, we will be within this group, and that is our reality.

[18]**God says** – My Son, Jesus Christ, will return soon. He has been here as a man and has done everything exactly as I told him, up to and including, [19]humbling himself to death for my lost creation. Some accept and believe in Him; many refuse my love. Sadly, in just the same way they refused to listen and went their own way when I made them. Most remain in refusal to this day. In the previous nine epochs of my dealing with my creation, [20]what they really wanted was to glory in themselves. Broadly speaking, they are still of much the same opinion, as they insist on their way. [21]Because they refuse to accept the truth, the delusion and deception which is starting to overtake them is now rapidly spreading – even across the whole world. I have always continued bringing people to myself, but [22]the open and free offer of my love was never planned to last indefi-

nitely - [23]I am going to conclude it [24]with the return of my only Son Jesus, whom I have appointed as judge of all, as he is also human. It has not happened until it happens. [25]So, at this point, I can still say "Come, put your trust in my Son while you are living and there is still time to do so."

A thought to consider: What is truth? Let's look at three constants:

1. The boiling point for water at sea level is 100 C (degrees centigrade) or 212 F (Fahrenheit)

2. The speed of sound at sea level is 761 mph or 1225 km/h

3. The speed of light in a vacuum is 186,000 mps or 300,000 km/s

We would not consider altering these values. They are fixed points comparatively recently discovered, and like many other laws governing our everyday lives and the universe, they are known to be 100% reliable – we have evidence for this.

In these and many other examples, we can conclude that if what is claimed to be the case is substantiated by evidence, we have truth. However, generally speaking in our world today, truth is not spoken of in these terms. Many now say there is no such thing as truth. Rather, truth is relative. This means that what is true for today may not be so for tomorrow due to changing circumstances, or my truth may not be your truth, meaning what works for me, may not work for you. This modern view proposes that we modify 'truth' to meet changing circumstances. Under this view, truth is no longer absolute, but merely a shifting idea or changeable theory. But this defies logic and common sense. Truth, by its very nature, is absolute. The fundamentals of truth can't change – true north or true south do not alter and are 100% reliable, as are the three examples given to show the accuracy of truth.

Why then should we feel that God, the maker of these laws would alter his universal plan for the eternal wellbeing of mankind, when he already tells us in the Word of Life that [26]"God so loved the world that he gave his only Son, that whoever believes in him will not be lost, but will have everlasting life." Jesus says, [27]"I am the way and the truth, and the life. No one comes to the Father except through me".

In light of this, how can all paths of sincere belief lead to God, when he tells us his way for us is through his son Jesus, and it is the only way that leads to life?

14

LIFE – NO GUESSING GAME

Now as the reader, whilst you may not personally identify with any of the commonly accepted responses of wider humanity as outlined, here we have the picture - God says the way he sees things, but we say the way we see them is different. Countless numbers of people have tried to disprove the nine events mentioned ending up with numerous theories. Many highly regarded students of scepticism in their quest to discredit, have like "doubting Thomas" become believers in Jesus Christ as Lord and God with life changing personal testimonies.

In the final event, we have the word of Jesus giving a guarantee that he will return. The God of history has already fulfilled to the letter nine out of nine previous events. In human terms when the score is nine out of nine, the tenth is presumed a certainty. However, when God says this, it can be guaranteed.

It is little wonder with all the coming and going of events and the number of generations involved, many highly qualified people, when asked the question "What is the meaning to life?", give the usual response, "We don't know."

Jesus Christ was in no such quandary. By contrast, he says the vital issue is to know God and Jesus Christ, the one whom He has sent. His life here was marked by outstanding miracles – the blind given sight, healing of incurable diseases and the dead raised back to life etc. These amazing acts gave clear evidence that he was both man and God. However, his main purpose on Earth was, and remains to this day, to give new life to all who will receive it. Again, in the Word of Truth, God in His love is saying to us, even today, if you will hear Jesus' voice, do not harden your hearts as some do. May you be blessed in these last days to accept Jesus as both your Saviour and Lord.

The truth is also clear, that while many now come to accept God and the offer of His only Son Jesus, most do not. The reality is that both ways cannot be true - one is, and one is not. This corresponds with Jesus' words: [1]"No one can serve two masters" and [2]"Those who are not for me are against me." There is no middle ground – we cannot have it both ways. Nearing the end of his 30 years, Jesus said to his followers, [3]"My peace I give to you, my peace I leave with you, I do not give to you as this world gives." After this came his crucifixion, his death, his resurrection, then his reappearance and after this, his departure from the world. His followers were commanded time and time again to stop telling people this message, but they said, [4]"We can only speak of what we have both seen and heard as eyewitnesses." They were prepared to die rather than deny, and the only reason they or indeed anyone, would go that far is because they were 100% convinced that the person they saw after the crucifixion was identical to and indeed the same one they had known and followed beforehand. He showed them his nail pierced hands and feet. They recognized his voice and shared food with him. That was enough. Each follower had a different life story of how they came to know the Lord, but they shared the same belief through faith in this incredible loving and forgiving God, in the person of Jesus, His death, His resurrection and His gift of eternal life.

The strong and convincing power for those who believed then, and now, came when the Holy Spirit entered the lives of the believers, together with the peace Jesus had promised. Though 2000 years have elapsed, it has been the same through each generation for those who put their trust in this risen Lord Jesus Christ. As it was then, so it is now; Christians (believers in Jesus) are not perfect. If anyone makes a judgement of God on this basis, they are mistaken. [5]God will never have to retract or withdraw his Word, but will we stay as we are or become serious with God? Just because we or others may say "He isn't here; He is irrelevant, or He doesn't exist", does it mean this is the truth just because we or someone says so? Shouldn't we consider that by comparison with His word of life, which stands the test of time, both we and those who appear certain without evidence are "here today and gone tomorrow"?

15

THE TIGHTROPE WALKER

In the late 1800's a famous tight rope walker was in Maryborough, Queensland, Australia. He strung a rope across the Mary River and asked the crowd, [1]"Do you think I can walk across the river?" The crowd responded excitedly, "Yes". He then brought out a wheelbarrow and asked, "Do you think I can wheel this across?" "Yes", again was the noisy response. Then, "Who will jump in the barrow and let me wheel them across?"

At this, the crowd went silent, until a young boy said, "I will". He climbed into the barrow and they successfully crossed the river to the roar of applause from the crowd. This young boy was my grandfather! The question, in essence, is the same today. God says He is holy, loving and forgiving. At great cost he paid the price for the going of our own way – it is commonly called sin.

The question is, who will believe? Who will step forward and trust what God says, gaining peace and security now and for eternity? It is a choice we all must make.

If, like myself, you find it hard or even impossible to believe, [2]ask and you will receive; look for God and you will find him, knock on his door and you will find the door will be opened to you. That is the door of faith, forgiveness, the peace of God and eternal life. Should you need further assurance, say like many have said before you, [3]"yes, Lord I do believe, help my unbelief!"

16

WHAT NEXT?

If after having read this word of life, you have now taken the step of faith as outlined, and accepted Jesus Christ to save you, there are three very important steps to further help and establish you in this new life which is life indeed.

1. Ask God to direct you to someone or a group of like-minded, understanding people who will help and strengthen you in your daily life with Jesus Christ and not your old self as master. Let me assure you, this does take some learning – it's a lifetime journey.
2. Pray with thankfulness that you will be able to share your decision in ways that will be helpful to others finding Jesus as you have (Don't just keep this good news to yourself).
3. Always remember in this new life, you have been eternally saved to love God and serve the interests of others. This is great news.

ABOUT THE AUTHOR

Sydney Hughes lives on the Sunshine Coast of Queensland, Australia, and is married to Pixie. He is retired from full-time work and this is his first book. He is passionate about the Christian faith and has a sincere desire to help others find the peace and joy that comes from knowing Jesus Christ.

NOTES

2. A Great Start - Major Event 1

1. Genesis 1:27

3. Catastrophic End - Major Event 2

1. Genesis 6:6-8
2. Genesis 7:7-24

4. Unfinished Project - Major Event 3

1. Genesis 11:4-5
2. Genesis 11:7-9
3. Genesis 1:28

5. People on the Move - Major Event 4

1. Psalm 19:1-4
2. Romans 1:21-22

6. The International Connection - Major Event 5

1. Genesis 12:1-5
2. Genesis 16:15, Genesis 21:1-4
3. Genesis 25:21-26
4. Genesis 35:9
5. Genesis 37:3
6. Genesis 41:9
7. Genesis 41:14
8. Genesis 41:41
9. Genesis 41:1-2
10. Genesis 45:1-5
11. Exodus 1:8-9

12. Exodus 3:7-9
13. Revelation 3:7

7. Slavery to Freedom - Major Event 6

1. Isaiah 55:8-9
2. Exodus 3:3
3. Exodus 4:13-14
4. Exodus 14:5-7
5. Exodus 14:13
6. Genesis 50:25-26
7. Exodus 13:19

8. Hitting a Brick Wall - Major Event 7

1. Exodus 20:1-17
2. Leviticus 18:5
3. Exodus 24:3
4. Judges 6:1-6
5. 1 Kings 18:17-18
6. Hebrews 13:8
7. Micah 5:2

9. Good News Arrives - Major Event 8

1. Micah 5:2
2. Hosea 11:1
3. Matthew 2:23, Isaiah 11:1
4. Luke 1:26-35; Matthew 1:18-25
5. Luke 2:4-5
6. Luke 2:6-7
7. Matthew 2:16
8. Matthew 2:13
9. Matthew 2:22-23
10. Luke 2:23
11. Luke 4:1-13
12. Luke 4:40-44
13. Luke 4:18-22
14. Luke 5:27-30
15. John 19:7
16. Matthew 26:63-65

17. Matthew 21:12
18. John 8:56
19. John8:44
20. Matthew 15:14
21. John 11:44-45
22. John 11:47-480
23. John 12:10
24. Matthew 26:15-16
25. Luke 23:13-15
26. John 10:17-18
27. Mark 8:31, Matthew 27:63
28. Romans 3-23
29. John 3:36, Romans 6:18-19
30. Luke 23:39
31. Luke 23:40
32. Luke 23:42
33. Luke 15:10
34. Ephesians 2:8-9
35. Romans 3:23
36. Hebrews 9:32
37. Mark 15:34
38. John 19:30
39. John 19:3
40. Matthew 27:13-14
41. Isaiah 11:9
42. Mark 3:23-26

10. The International Game Changer - Major Event 9

1. Matthew 28:18
2. 1 Corinthians 1:25
3. Mark 8:31
4. Matthew 26:32-35
5. John 20:9
6. Matthew 26:56
7. Matthew 27:57
8. Matthew 27:63
9. Matthew 28:2-4
10. Luke 24:4-8
11. Matthew 28:7-8
12. Matthew 28:10
13. 1 Corinthians 15:6

14. Luke 24:13-27, 31
15. John 20:24-29
16. John 20:17
17. John 14:25-27
18. Matthew 20:17, Luke 24:49
19. Romans 8:11
20. John 14:18-23
21. Luke 24:4-48
22. Luke 24:50
23. Matthew 28:11-15
24. Acts 2:2
25. Acts 2:3
26. Acts 2:7-8
27. Acts 2:13
28. Acts 2:14-24, Acts 2:32, Acts 2:36-40
29. Acts 2:42-47
30. Acts 4:1-2
31. Acts 8:14-15
32. Acts 7:58, Acts 9:1

11. The Ultimate Victory - Major Event 10

1. John 14:3
2. Matthew 24:3, 12,32, 35, Acts 1:6-9, Luke 24:44
3. Matthew 24:42-43
4. Matthew 5:18
5. Isaiah 53
6. 1 John 5:12
7. Isaiah 9:6-7
8. Matthew 1:21
9. Psalm 22:1
10. Psalm 22:14-15
11. Psalm 22:26
12. Psalm 22:27-28
13. Psalm 22:31
14. Revelation 22:12-13
15. Isaiah 44:6-9
16. Revelation 1:8, Isaiah 46:9
17. Luke 12:16-21
18. Mark 8:36
19. Matthew 24:3
20. Matthew 24:10-13
21. 2 Timothy 3:1

22. Luke 21:26
23. 2 Timothy 3:3
24. Matthew 24:7, Mark 13:15-20
25. Matthew 24:6
26. Luke 13:8
27. Daniel 12:4
28. Matthew 24:14
29. Luke 24: 33
30. Luke 23:28
31. Luke 13:34-38, Matthew 23:38-39
32. Revelation 13:4
33. Revelation 13:8
34. Revelation 13:6-18
35. Mark 13:20
36. Matthew 24:22, Mark 13:20
37. Revelation 9:20
38. Revelation 9:21
39. Luke 16:31
40. 2 Timothy 3:7
41. 2 Timothy 4:4
42. Matthew 33:35
43. Matthew 24:44
44. John 8:24
45. John 10:10
46. Isaiah 1:18
47. 2 Corinthians 6:2
48. John 6:35-37
49. 2 Corinthians 5:17
50. Revelation 22:20

12. Testimony – Light in the Darkness

1. 1 Peter 3:18
2. Hebrews 11:6
3. Matthew 7:7-8, Luke 11:9-10
4. 2 Corinthians 5:17
5. John 16:8
6. 1 John 3:8
7. Mark 14:36
8. Romans 8:35
9. Psalm 130:4
10. John 1:12
11. 1 Peter 2:24-25

12. John 10:27-28
13. Mark 2:7-10
14. Hebrews 4:12-13

13. Fact or Fiction

1. Isaiah 53:6
2. Genesis 6:6
3. Genesis 11:4
4. Genesis 11:8
5. Genesis 12:1-5
6. Exodus 3:7-10
7. Exodus 34:10
8. Isaiah 56:8
9. 2 Kings 17:38-41
10. 1 John 4:14
11. Luke 2:11
12. Matthew 3:17
13. 1 Timothy 1:15-16
14. Romans 8:32
15. Romans 1:4
16. Romans 8:38-39
17. Luke 24:46-47
18. Revelation 22:7-10
19. Philippians 2:6-11
20. Philippians 3:18-19
21. 2 Thessalonians 2:10-11
22. Hebrews 3:7
23. Genesis 6:3
24. 2 Corinthians 5:10
25. Hebrews 4:7
26. John 3:16
27. John 14:6

14. Life – No Guessing Game

1. Luke 16:13
2. Matthew 12:30
3. John 14:27
4. Acts 4:20
5. Matthew 24:35

15. The Tightrope Walker

1. James 1:22-25, James 2:19
2. Matthew 7:7-8
3. Mark 9:23-24